Of Things Visible and Invisible

Of Things Visible and Invisible

POEMS

S.H. LONG

author**HOUSE**

AuthorHouse™
1663 Liberty Drive
Bloomington, IN 47403
www.authorhouse.com
Phone: 833-262-8899

Published by AuthorHouse 04/08/2021

ISBN: 978-1-4969-5129-8 (sc)
ISBN: 978-1-4969-5128-1 (e)

Library of Congress Control Number: 2014919472

Print information available on the last page.

Dedicated to the beautiful
lives of
the author's son
and the artist's mother;

Claxton Allen Long, Jr.
and
Roann M. Schweitzer

pax

CONTENTS

GRATITUDE

To God, for guiding me always, especially through the last thirty years. During this time of ongoing formation He has led me to the Catholic Church and the Dominican Order of which I am a member in the St. Albert the Great Chapter of Dominican Laity in Oakland, CA.

To Marcy, who has been my most ardent and exceptional editor here in San Francisco.

To Mary, who edited my last book, *An Errant Design*, and has graciously continued from New York to most skillfully oversee this present project of putting my poetry into print.

To Debra, in Ohio, for the beauty of her exquisite art.

To Marcy, Mary, and Debra for the honor and delight of their friendship over and above their talents.

To my beloved daughter whose love and encouragement delight my heart and whose very presence gives me heavenly joy.

"...Beauty and Poetry are an inexorable absolute which requires a total gift of oneself and which suffers no division. Only with God can a man give himself totally *twice at the same time*, first to his God and second to something which is a reflection of his God."

Jacques Maritain

PROLOGUE

This book fulfills nearly a lifetime of hope. A hope of one day sharing abroad some of the visible and invisible things that the eyes of my heart notice, contemplate, love, and interpret. Perhaps one could call these poems translations, translations of experiences into a language that captures the beauty of their essence. Even this simple description opens itself up to myriad connotations. Language often confronts us with such enormous limitations.

The kind of language that is needed to translate the essence of an experience into poetry is a bit like brain surgery in a field hospital with all the distinct inadequacies. The doctor finds the traces of brokenness in order to restore the original health and beauty of a person's body. A poet also requires traces. Wielding words, the poet makes present the essence of what he sees and contemplates from the raw material, beauty, and brokenness, in order to reflect another kind of beauty.

Poetry emanates from the heart. The heart, being made by the Creator, needs something *other* to capture an experience, a moment. Not all things are beautiful in and of themselves, but poetry is ever on a mission. Its desire is to reflect, to love the innate beauty that all created *things* reveal in some way, no matter their apparent distortion whether seen or unseen.

Many experiences are tiny, fleeting ones, others are huge and overwhelming. Most experiences happen on an inner plane, some reaching a pitch that need expression, need sharing. To express those *things*, like the rigid poise of a hummingbird or a loved ones' passing, become ennobled through poetry. Poetry communicates from the depths to the depths.

In the end, poems live by being read. The reader loves them into life, resuscitates their words right off the page and extracts all that resonates. I only wish I could be reading these poems for the first time.

I

Floating particles of fragrance
Signal my attention
As I perceive whispered prayers
Like strings of an instrument
Fashioned from voices
That reveal Christ's passion
For tenderness

ASHES

Gulls swoop
Like flying scrimshaw
Sliding on
Ash-tipped wings,
Feather-edged driftwood,
Grey moon
Eclipsed down
To its wink-white breast
Soft in the winter's
Night sky

Gulls soar daily
Smooth as ivory needles
Stringing days
Into years
Of chalcedony beads
Fingering Advent, Lent, Easter.

REMEMBERING

Three-toed clouds queued and hovered
While I piled the car with
Memorabilia
Too sacred to sell.
A poem by my great-grandmother
About Kansas and alfalfa
Beside me sat my Mother
Holding pictures of my children
Rattling in frames
On a tear-stained pillow.
In the backseat a lamp,
A blue silk foot stool and
Photo portraits of me
Looking into now
Typing in dark glasses
To bear the light.

WHY

O, Lord, do You ordain
That we should crush You
To be one with You
Must You endure destruction
After consecration
To fulfill oblation
Let me not be the cause of more pain
How can I be Your gentle dove of love
And yet trample You behind my open lips

ONE FEATHER

One feather is torn
My boy, my
Inimitable boy
Taken like a down quill
From my roosting breast
A ragged hole
Filled with emptiness

GRIEF

Grief screams
Where is my love
My darling one
My baby

In the end
It submits to love
Crushed by
Barefooted hope

DECEMBER

Dark gray
Heavy
The color of wartime
Ashes
Ancient debris
Fills the belly
Of a winter hung
Pity flung
Moon
Over a house gutted
With Christmas longing

MARINA SKY

The morning stretches
Seamless as an egg
Damp air breaks cool
Across my face

As impertinent reminders
Of the absent yolk
Intrude on my metaphor
Like single poppies
Among weeds

Stray eucalyptus leaves
Curve in quiet affinity
With the concrete sidewalk
I think of stable straw

Mary would have been
Five months with child by now
I share that dark space
Waiting to be born

If I could crack open
A piece of sky
Would the edges crowd with doves?
Would they watch the blue
Pour through like liquid
Coming to fill my heart?

NIGHT CORNERS

Ragged edges of night
Wedge and jam into corners of my room
Stubborn, sullen
Persistent in assaulting silence

How dare you crowd me
With piled up sins
In the same room where epiphany trembles
Like aspen leaves

In the morning
A moth flicks dust
On last night's gloom

PILGRIM CRANE

Formation, like a paper crane
creased and flattened,
hid my light,
it folded over, out of sight,
only absence remained
rough textured, cold
turned over, bent, pushed, hurt.
Shadows gathered in places that used to shine.
I want to retreat,
I want to reform,
opposing corners
quick, take cover!
I'll never be the same,
"Origami!"
Like a cry for help in *crane*.
Don't leave me familiar self,
I don't want to be new without You.
Stay in my folds.
It's too hard to be alone,
a kite without a cord.
I'm turning inside out

with no shape or direction,
my legs are gone.
I feel a pressing hard against my back now
with mighty thumbs
shaping small stubs,
a pilgrim crane getting wings?
Will I ever fly? Where would I go?
Into the eye of the sun
hot with love,
breath of God
ignite me.

PILGRIM CRANE SEQUEL

In August I think of Mary.
What size would she have been by now?
At five months
She herself just a child.

Leaves still dreaming in green
Wave slowly to December
While a new song rustles
In their throat, swaying.

Mary is my companion,
A friend in formation,
Being born and giving birth,
Becoming and leaving behind.

Nothing ahead cancels this hour,
Nothing before or after.
We are simply here, now, waiting
Doubled over in the pain of good-byes.

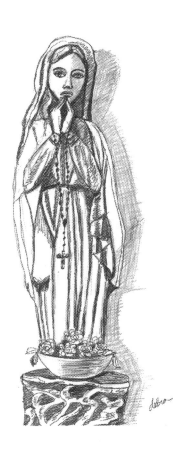

II

A wreath of voices prays the Rosary
Intoning a love song in musical courtship
Its cadence is like the coruscating flames of candlelight
Wafting in a warm prism of desire that rises in praise
Over heads bowed down in wonder

CONNECTICUT VIEW

Starlings spill
  Into the sky
    Living tea leaves
      Swirling with fall breeze
    Stirring red seas
  Parting dry leaves
 Meeting my eye
Angel still

HAIKU TRILOGY

A half hung moon slips
Through the day
Sheer as cloud
While the stars are sleeping

Tall palm leaves bend and sway
In pairs
Like courting swans
Playing in the wind

Empty nest
Emptiness
Feathers in a teacup
Where are my children

INNER SPACE

A whirl of space
In a separate universe
Floats quiet as terrestrial dust
Inside a quarry
Marked by skin and bone

Bursting through these spatial aisles
Streams a sphere of bright nuptial satin
Lustrous as a jewel, a pearl, a face

SPRING WAVE

Butterfly wings bear
Down in the heat
Like rice paper fans
Cooling my eyes

Blue fastens thick and hot
On a wall of eucalyptus trees
Waiting for sea winds
To lick their leaves green

With the precision of a hummingbird
The evening ball of earth rests for a moment
In a ring of yellow light
While night unlaces her moist creamy stars

ACACIA

Spring acacia bleeds through the streets,

nailed quiet
to ground cracks
cotton whispers
shadow soft
huddled
still as mice
wedged cold
out of the sun's
eye
looking for
Sunday.

JUNE

Birdsong steps
Slippery
Through late afternoon
A humming
Rides the air like
Sunlight
On grazing sheep

Clouds
Still as orchids
Fill
My window
A latticed screen
Measures each
Drop
Of nightfall
As it pours
Down
Quiet as grass

Am I praying?

JULY

Startling bird songs
Cat walk a tune
Along clay baked rooftops
Whistling mood tones down
To the dawn scented light

A new wisp of moon nests
In that thin steep blue
As it rides on the rounding
Loop of day

Subtle steaming air swells
Into a waiting night
And cool brushes by
With her long lashed stars

ONE HOST

Round as a petal
Thin as an eyelash
Contains the love that made the Moon
Dearest Moon-maker
No effort mars Your gift
Nothing can convey
Moments with You
And nothing compares
To Your holy name
So Compelling, so mild
How could I ever leave You

TREASURE

Once when I was little
My Mother took me to the beach
I saw a glistening pink starfish
Making polka dots in the sand
As it inched beside the foam-fringed sea
I asked if I could take it home
And she said, "yes"
Her answer was always "yes"

My new pet starfish
Was to live in the basement
On a stool I reached the faucet to fill my pail
I poured water all over the floor
And watched my pet slowly move
It stopped being pink and glistening
There was no salt in the water
Or sunshine or sand
Or food for a starfish to eat
Being little I didn't think of those things
Or of the heater or linoleum floor
And soon I forgot my beautiful treasure altogether

Now I am old
And my treasure is You
What if I brought You home
Without consuming You at Mass
And held You on the table where I pray
We could never be any closer that way
Just imagine such a terrible thought

Only to be received and hidden
Deep inside of me
Can You remain my treasure
Kept outside of me like the starfish
I become a pirate, a looter
Beauty taken is love forsaken

PRAYER

It seems so effortless
For birds to be
Transcendent
Sparrows, sea gulls
The wild parrot that comes
Some mornings like
A jade green almond eye
In the face of my garden
Looking like grace
All gleaming and smooth

How can I offer
What I can't bring near
When words fall short
Of the wind-traced light

Then night looks down
Like the inside
Of a freshly opened indigo gourd
Silently exposing a secret sky
Dripping wet white stars
From its cool prayer-swept skin

RIVER OF NIGHT

A sunset regatta of clouds
Sailed past a spectator moon
Huge shell-shaped petals
Silver-edged eddies
Catch on the river of night

The sound of immensity
Silent as breath
Slipped across my face
Answering the question
Of their source and destination
"They are one,"
That's what it said to me
To me and the runnel-faced moon

NEW LIVES

"They shall spring up like a green tamarisk,
like willows by flowing streams." Isaiah 44:4

And they come even among the dry and dying
star-plated, shimmering
skin greener than goodness
newborn leaves whir
hungry, about to be wild.

They spread like jam
over toast-colored branches
like fat little feet
they outgrow today
and after that tomorrow.

III

Whispered prayers thread
Through pure smoky billows
As grace reaches out
With fingers of bread and wine
To fill me beyond all telling

EASTER CANDLE

Easter candle, staff of light
Cylinder of triumph
Sign of the Kingdom
Inviting the lost
Illumining the found
Towering lustrous wax
Burnished sun-oiled skin
Glistening like an athlete
Pointing, stretching, straining
Soaring from a center shaft of shadow
Growing ever brighter
On either side
Till a sudden bloody highlight
From a ruby-throated window
Blisters and bursts on its skin
As it meets the Source of Life

"In him was life, and the life was the light of men."

WITH YOU

INRI
With You
Anything could happen
It's expected
Word
Light
Life
Angel
Birth
Blood
Pearl
Fire
Water
Sight
Bread
Wine
Church
Kingdom
Love
Joy
Anything could happen. It's expected
You are the Morning Star
The incandescent Flame of Love

SACRED MOMENTS

Your voice, Lord, is feather soft.
It rests warmly behind my eyes,
Down in the back of my throat
To my heart.
You enter me crisp, astounding.
An issue of blood attends Your sweet body,
And makes us one.
Moist, warm, the taste of heaven,
You complete me without a sound.

TABLE

Your table teems with love
Pouring thick and round
Toward the edges
Its surface is glazed
With the luster of dawn.

LENT

Lenten Lover
Softly waiting
Pale and calm
The accident of Your hidden appearance
Is almost exceeded
By a silver gleam

Yet as You caress me
My breath touches You
All my senses are alert
I hear Your silence
I feel Your nearness
I receive Your pierced body
Taste Your Eucharistic presence
Here is Your divine face
We kiss
We are one

PARTAKING

Dry, flat, crisp and sharp
What I consume
Cool, wet, smooth, becoming
Warm, even stinging
Spreading its content like a hum
O, the taste and feel of Your body and blood
It opens cool then rises in warmth
Reaching to a peak of certainty
That You are in residence
Slowly You settle
Into a holy sepulcher
Your flesh in my flesh
O, God, let us never be parted
Linger, my Love

GLEAM

A gleam
A star-white shaft
Pierces heaven
And lands
On a linen-shrouded table
Such affinity for the wood beneath
A holiness mark of the God-man
My Lenten Lover

Though I am so unworthy
Let at least my eyelids
Capture Your face
And bring You home to me

BLESSED SACRAMENT

Blessed Sacrament
Translucent with the Son
A momentary universe
Raised high
Above my waiting hands

Worlds and stars
Swirled through this multiverse
Lit by countless suns
Dots of blue
Pulsing particles
Specks of life

All in an instant
Like love at first sight

EUCHARIST

Shadows on the Host trace
    His thorn-pierced head
Splashed on the Chalice
    His white robed torso rises up
Extending a morsel from the gleam

A membrane between heaven and earth
    Splinters open
And a knowing enters me
    Smooth as silver

LACEY SHADOWS

Lacey shadows fall
Under the sweet sounds of liturgy
They trace Your adorable face
On the Blessed Sacrament
As it is held high

On the Chalice
A white light is born on the silver surface
Your gleaming body
Rises and reaches
As it is held above

Just light and shadow
Playing with my imagination
Yet so near, so real
Just steps away
From where I kneel

My heart and mind strain
Pressing down on my breath
Stretching through my eyes

Like frantic arms
To find and hold You
Like Magdalene
So present, so near
Such longing

"O, Lord, I am not worthy."
"Beloved, you are mine."

IV

Whirling lustrous fragrance
Floats hidden inside
Sheer particles of incense
Twirling toward the light like tulle
Tender as the Bridegroom

MORNING PRAYER

Low circular chapel sounds
Of praying Rosaries
Roll through an open door
Into the choir stalls
They join the stony echoes of
Sandaled footsteps scuffing across marble
Amongst the ping of wooden beads
Swinging softly
Against long chalky habits
Each sound rises up
To meet the Son
As He awakens the jewel-spangled
Windows

AMEN

All beauty, truth, and love
Wait for me
My meal, my life
How much of me do You need?
Just my Amen?

And how indeed do You enter?
Do you dive in
Muscle in
Or spread in like honey
Slow, rounded, spiraling
Constant, sparkling
Amber glowing essence
Filling?

Scourged shoulders gleam whitely divine
How do you become You?
No matter
It is You
That's all in all.

MY GIVEN

A language from the stars
    Whispers to my soul
    Does it want me or
    Just the darkness

It spills, gushing in
    Then its radiance
    Lingers
    Like eternity

Heartland, you are my language
    You are mine, given me
    Say you'll never
    Leave

These words bring me to the vast
    Miniature interior
    That seems to have no end
    But in You

ADORATION

"His splendor spreads like the light
Rays shine far from beside him."
                    Habakkuk 3:3

A silent fire of love shines
On invisible radiance
Reaching for the sweet moon
Of accidental bread
Godhead
Exquisite gazing

Sun setting with crescent shadow
Smiles
Whispering
"All shall be well,
And all shall be well
And all manner of thing shall be well."

ESSENCE

This morning I felt Your warmth
All virile and golden
Spreading Your essence
Vibrant across my lips
Then time cooled it
To a glassy sea

Later and last in line
A poor adoring procession
Walked in haste
To place Your face into a crown

Softly startling
Our silent watch resumes
You in me and I in You
A star, a spark
A fresh exchange of love
In celestial swaths of light

Velvet harmony
Soundless hymn
Sweet Essence, stay
Stay on

PROOF

Are pages of scientific proof of Your death
Clear photos of Your Shroud and Sudarium
With carbon dating and blood tests
More real, more holy, more true
Than one consecrated host
Enclosed behind glass
Within a golden Monstrance

They are not the same
Nor are they equal
Instead I fall prostrate
Before the perfect mystery of each

JUST OVER THERE

Just over there is Your presence
Here…there…
And everywhere
It floats, hovers, shines and sings
It creaks and pings
Darts and brings
Light sparkling things
That glitter and glow.

They blow
Words into flight
L•e•t•t•e•r•s
Black and white.

They shoot and scatter
Bounce up and gather
Dissolve into matter
Straining for release
Rolling out of reach
Mercurial, elusive words
Flying away
With all I want to say
Love, Love, Love

INWARD SIGHT

When I close my eyes
A gleaming atmosphere
Blazes with a billion granular lights
A miniature starry night
Bursts from my inward sight
Tiny stars spackled against a translucent night
Dazzling lusters that pulse with all their might
Teeming in full flight
To glimpse the mysterious sight
Of Your eternal beauty

Inside this finite world
My heart is hurled
Your quiet figure has me gripped
Like silk across my lips

LITURGY

Sacred Liturgy: alive, real
Bursting with infinitely faceted purpose
An operatic ballet
Of adoration

Interspersed shadows enfold
Scattered radiances
That strain to shape Your face
I search through these table signs

Signatures of natural science
Make visible
The revealed truth
My heart already knows

BEAUTY

Sometimes beauty is too staggering
to bear
it is always more than itself
bringing universes
unrelated
toppling
in transparent traces
ineffable, eternal.

All wedged tight into a moment
to retain and revisit.
Still it is only a moment
not the beauty.

SLEEP

Before sleep came
My day tried vainly
To reassemble itself
In coruscating pixels
Throbbing to find
Their places in time
Morning brushed
Silently around
The corners of my room
Sweeping them all into
Yesterday

ADORATION II

Shoots of gold, scattered shadows
house You entirely
Silence embraces our communion,
union, a womb of exchanging
charged with Your love
with our pitiful offering
desperate needs and last hope
pray, conform, they believe
let me know what they appear to have
what they see,
am I doing it right
is this adoration or doubt
let me never bring dishonor
from my punctured heart

A NEW FIRST FRIDAY

Luster of light and love linger loosely
there You are right before me
You are the same
with soft countenance
quiet, peaceful, Son of Mary,
Son of sons.
But I, have I changed
more in love or less
mercurial, measured by time
I am closer to death
fear is gone
instead You fill me
In thy mercy stay
not that death is near
but that your love is all in all

SACRAMENT II

Reproducing, deducing
Your suffering and Your death
above the silent sacrament
sequestered in a looking glass
translates into a living heart
within my own
eternal, silent as air
a life more real pulses
hidden in my breast
time is absent
only love remains
in review it's just a moment
a gleaming ornament
now a soft new hue

RED FLAME OF PRESENCE

Red flame of presence
presents the pale Host on view
embraced by brass
that mirrors the light
residing in You.
Earthen angels attend
while all is silent
as countless prayers burst
within each quiet chest
still as orchids
that stretch along their branches
cool they live in beauty
within a marble chapel
more air than matter
like a soul within a body
Son of Man Your traces are everywhere
while still we look through
a jumble of treasures
to find a face so like our own
but is completely new

MIRROR

A marble wall mirrors the flame.
Will I ever mirror You?
Like marble I am cold, lifeless,
self-contained
with nothing to give,
only empty show
veins with no blood
You alone give me life.
In perfect stillness
peace is defined,
resting in silence
while the hope of prayer
sluices invisibly
through the hum
of internal prayer.

NOTES

Title is taken from the Nicene Creed.

Page xiii: Maritain, Jacques. *Responsibility of the Artist.* New York: Charles Scribner's Sons, 1960.

Page 15   "Marina Sky." *Reformed Journal*, 1989.

Page 29   "Haiku Trilogy." *The First Press*, Summer 1989.

Page 35   "Acacia." *Reformed Journal*, April 1989: 18.

Page 37   "June." *Reformed Journal*, June 1989.

Page 47   "Prayer." *The First Press*, March 1991.

Page 51   "New Lives." Isaiah 44:4 NRS

Page 55   "Easter Candle." John 1:4 RSV

Page 85   "Adoration." Habakkuk 3:3 NAB

Page 85   "All shall be well—" quote Dame Juliana of Norwich.

All proceeds from this book will go to fund:

> The Claxton Allen Long, Jr. Burse
> St. Albert's Priory
> Western Dominican Province
> 5890 Birch Court
> Oakland, CA 94618

This is the scholarship S. H. Long set up in her son's memory for the education and formation of Dominican priests. This Burse was started from the proceeds of her first book, *An Errant Design*.

ABOUT THE AUTHOR

Having lived in New York and Europe, S.H. Long returned
home to San Francisco, where she now enjoys two little Maltese
dogs and a lovely garden, and lives as a Lay Dominican. This
selection of poems reflects a life journey through seasons of
loss to new beginnings.

ABOUT THE ILLUSTRATOR

Debra Classen was born in San Diego, California and currently lives in Cleveland, Ohio with her husband, Dr. Roger Classen. Debra became a self-taught artist, sharing the beauty of form through mostly watercolors and acrylics. She also has an M.A. in Counseling and an M.A. in theology from Saint Mary's Seminary.

Her faith and studies, as well as the creative and healing force of art in her own life, became the impetus for the founding of the non-profit ministry, "The Mute Swan," which she and her husband began ten years ago. Their mission is to help others "discover hope and healing through God's Beauty in our world."

To learn more about the ministry visit their web page: www. muteswan.org.

To read the daily meditations, reflections, prayers and art visit their Facebook page: www.facebook.com/The Mute Swan.

Printed in the United States
by Baker & Taylor Publisher Services